STEAM NOSTALGIA IN THE NORTH OF ENGLAND

Paul Hurley and Philip Braithwaite

About the Authors

Paul Hurley is a writer and author and a member of the Society of Authors. He has contributed to numerous railway and other magazines and written twenty-three local history books and an award-winning novel. He is married to Rose and lives in Winsford, Cheshire.

Philip Braithwaite has been a railway photographer since the late 1950s, spending time in South Africa photographing the last of the steam traction there. Upon returning from South Africa, he continued his love of all things steam by bringing with him his Thomas Green & Son 1924 steam roller and living van. Philip lives in Barnton, Cheshire, with his wife Helen.

Front Cover Top: Royal Scot Class 4-6-0 No. 46144 *Honourable Artillery Company* leaves Patricroft station with a Liverpool–Newcastle train in the summer of 1960.

Front Cover Bottom: Jinty LMS 0-6-0 tank No. 47668 is seen shunting at Bank Quay station, Warrington, in 1962.

Back Cover: Dallam Shed, Warrington in 1964.

First published 2017

Amberley Publishing
The Hill, Stroud
Gloucestershire, GL5 4EP

www.amberley-books.com

Copyright © Paul Hurley and Philip Braithwaite, 2017

The rights of Paul Hurley and Philip Braithwaite to be identified as the Authors of this work have been asserted in accordance with the Copyrights, Designs and Patents Act 1988.

ISBN 978 1 4456 6200 8 (print)
ISBN 978 1 4456 6201 5 (ebook)

All rights reserved. No part of this book may be reprinted or reproduced or utilised in any form or by any electronic, mechanical or other means, now known or hereafter invented, including photocopying and recording, or in any information storage or retrieval system, without the permission in writing from the Publishers.

British Library Cataloguing in Publication Data.
A catalogue record for this book is available from the British Library.

Typesetting by Amberley Publishing.
Printed in the UK.

Introduction

From the dawning of the Railway Age in the early 1800s with the Stockton & Darlington Railway to those pivotal days in August 1968, when the final nail was slammed home in the coffin of main line steam traction, the North played a major role. Crown Street was the original terminus at the Liverpool end of the Liverpool & Manchester Railway, but it was soon superseded by the new Lime Street station. It was from Crown Street that Stephenson's *Rocket* left for Liverpool Road station in Manchester, now incorporated into the Museum of Science and Industry, as part of the Rainhill Trials. These trials occurred when the line opened on 6 October 1829. The *Rocket* won the trial by virtue of the fact that it was the only locomotive to complete it. A year later, when the line was opened, the MP for Liverpool, William Husskison, was struck by the *Rocket* and died of his injuries. The Duke of Wellington, who was the Prime Minister, was one of the witnesses to this tragedy.

However, onwards to The Grand Junction Railway (GJR), which by 1840 had taken over the Liverpool & Manchester Railway and would soon become the London & North Western Railway (LNWR). It became quite evident in those early days that railways were more than a fad. The GJR decided that what it needed was a factory to manufacture railway locomotives and all of the other paraphernalia for this new transport system. Edge Hill in Liverpool already had a railway facility, including Edge Hill station, the oldest passenger station in the world that is still in use today. It was from here that the Grand Junction recruited their first members of staff.

To house them, 200 cottages were built in the small village of Monks Coppenhall, soon to be incorporated into what was another small village, called Crewe. It is here that what was to become the huge Crewe Railway Works was built, which, during its long life, would build some 7,000 steam locomotives and at its height employ 40,000 people. By 1957 the works also built diesel locomotives; however, in 2005 it had fewer than 1,000 employees and that figure has dropped even further now, with the works a shadow of its former self. Most of the works have now gone to make way for other things. So the North of England could arguably be called the birthplace of the railways in Britain and probably the world. Crewe station has also been a major hub and still is. In this book we shall look at original steam traction in the region from the 1950s to the end of steam.

During the war years the railways were worked into the ground and after the war action was required. The new Labour government decided that to convert the rolling stock to diesel and electric was beyond the purse strings; coal was also still relatively cheap. So, despite the availability of alternative power, they did not follow most of Europe but remained with steam. Orders were placed for new steam engines and rolling stock, and thousands more were built up to 1960. What a brilliant thing to have happened for rail enthusiasts. In those far-off days, just about every schoolboy, and a lot of schoolgirls, were trainspotters. That is now a word that has been brought into disrepute somewhat and, as a result, it has changed into the more acceptable term of 'rail enthusiast'. But what fantastic days they were, with many different classes, some old and some new, to be spotted at wonderfully smoky and gritty stations with a smell like no other. Then there were the shed visits, clambering over the giant monsters with their smoke, steam, oil, and muck. Without that monumental decision to stick with steam in the 1940s, at least for a while anyway, young lives of the period would not have been enhanced to such an extent, and sitting by the trackside would never have been the same.

This book contains the photographs by Philip Braithwaite, a man who has enjoyed photographing British and South African steam traction for many years. Here, we look at the period from the late 1950s to the end of steam on northern rails in August 1968. Within these pages, you will find around 180 photographs of steam and a few diesel and electric locomotives in the North that have never been published before. There are a few that show steam engines in all of their vibrant lined black, BR green and carmine red, but not that many. We are looking here towards the end of steam in the North, a time when the care of locomotives was no longer a priority and dirty drab black and leaking steam prevailed.

As August 1968 approached, the love of steam did not wane. In fact, it increased greatly, and once again we saw the odd seemingly well cared for locomotive. A bit deceptive perhaps as this cleaning, polishing and painting of the buffers was mainly done by a hardy band of enthusiasts, sometimes behind the back of the shedmaster! It was a period following the industrial vandalism of Dr Richard Beeching and a time when there was a mass culling of steam engines, some with low mileage and just a few years since their first allocation. All of the photographs, but one, were taken by Philip Braithwaite, so enjoy them and drift back to an era of smoke, steam, soot and grime, and what an eclectic era it was. The shed numbers given were in the main those that were used at nationalisation.

A3 4-6-2 No. 60048 *Doncaster*

It is May 1963, and the station pilot at Doncaster station is Gresley 4-6-2 No. 60048. This was once a greyhound of the main line or, should I say, racehorse, as it was, like its stable mates, named not after Doncaster Works or town, but a racehorse called Doncaster who won the 1873 Epsom Derby. It was built on 30 August 1924 at Doncaster Works and now approaches Doncaster station doing the duty of a humble station pilot. The engine was ending its working days here, as less than four months later, it would be withdrawn and cut up at Doncaster Works on 8 September 1963.

Black Five 4-6-0 No. 45104

Black Five No. 45104 forges up the bank over the Twelve Arches near Warrington and on up to Moore. The engine sends out plenty of smoke and is certainly under pressure, despite the assistance of a 0-6-0 banker at the rear. The year is 1965 and the engine is, cosmetically at least, in very good condition. The engine was built at the Vulcan Foundry in Newton-le-Willows in May 1935. In May 1948, it could be found at 26B Agecroft; its last shed was 26C Agecroft, from where it was withdrawn on 30 June 1968 – just under two months before the end of steam on BR. It was scrapped by Cohen's of Kettering in October of that year.

Fairburn 2-6-4 tank No. 42189

It is 1965 and No. 42189 acts as station pilot at Leeds City station, designed by Charles E. Fairburn and based on the earlier Stanier LMS 2-6-4T. It had a taper boiler and shorter wheelbase and was built at Derby Works on 24 December 1947 and sent to 56F Low Moor. It ended its days at 20D Normanton, from where it was sent to Cashmores of Great Bridge on 30 September 1967 and scrapped nine months later.

LNER 04s 2-8-0 No. 63575 and WD 2-8-0

In the bleak mid-winter the snow is falling as No. 63575 and an unidentified WD 2-8-0 await attention, or an overhaul, at Gorton Locomotive Works, Manchester, in 1962. This shot shows just how bleak and cold loco yards were during winter in the days of steam. No. 63575 was designed by Edward Thompson; it was introduced in 1944 and rebuilt with a boiler designed by John G. Robinson when he was CME of the Great Central Railway. Thompson was CME of the LNER from 1941 to 1946. The first allocation on nationalisation was 38B Annesley, but I don't have the date of withdrawal for the locomotive.

Steam Nostalgia in the North of England

Crewe Works Fowler 0-6-0 Shunter

There is no number here; instead, we have a view of the jack of all trades in the railway sheds and yards. This one is a really rough engine, even for these end of steam days. This type was designed by Henry Fowler for the LMS and was nicknamed, among other things, 'Duck Sixes', because of the wheel arrangement. All were withdrawn between 1959 and 1966, with just three being preserved.

Britannia Class 4-6-2 No. 70025 *Western Star*

The first of two sightings of this locomotive: on this occasion, it is seen in 1966 picking up water over the Moore troughs, south of Warrington. Built in September 1952 and withdrawn in December 1967, the class was designed by Robert Riddles. The naming of the class after British historical figures came about as a result of a suggestion by well-known rail enthusiast Bishop Eric Treacy. *Western Star* was one of those named after stars, while a few others were named after Scottish lochs. Sadly, of this beautiful class, only two survived into preservation: Nos 70000 *Britannia* and 70013 *Oliver Cromwell*.

Britannia Class 4-6-2 No. 70028 *Royal Star*

Steam is coming to an end, and this powerful Britannia Class engine has lost its name plates as it leaves Acton Bridge station on the West Coast Main Line for the north in 1967. It was built on 27 October 1952 at Crewe Works, its first shed being 86C Cardiff Canton. No. 70028 was one of the Britannias that lost its smoke deflector full handrails after they proved a hazard to visibility of the drivers. It was withdrawn from 68A Carlisle Kingmoor on 16 September 1967 and broken up at J. McWilliams, Shettleston, on 17 January 1968.

Black Five 4-6-0 No. 45104

Now one of the ubiquitous Black Fives, in this case No. 45104, heads towards Chester at Arpley, Warrington, in 1964. It was built at the Vulcan Foundry on 31 May 1935, one of the large class of engines that numbered 842, built between 1934 and 1951. Designed by Stanier, in the early days they were known as Black Staniers, but this evolved into the Black Five. Eighteen members of the class have been preserved, but not this one. Its 1947 shed was 26B Agecroft and its last one 26C Bolton, from where it was dispatched for scrapping at Cohen's of Kettering on 31 October 1968.

Gresley K1 Class 2-6-0 No. 62054

Seen in steam at the Doncaster Loco shed in May 1963, it was built on 11 October 1949 at the North British Locomotive Company in Glasgow; it was designed by Arthur Peppercorn to a Gresley design, Sir Nigel Gresley having died suddenly in 1941. The locomotive had its last works visit in 1962 when it left the works after a general service on 4 May 1962. Its last shed was 36E Retford from where it was withdrawn on 20 December 1964 and was cut up the following May at Hughes Bolckow, Battleship Wharf, North Blyth.

Britannia Class 4-6-2 No. 70046 *Anzac*

In those long gone spotting days, this engine was listed in my Ian Allan *ABC* as an unnamed Brit. But I spotted that the new name *Anzac* had been affixed. Named after the Australian and New Zealand troops, the engine heads southbound towards Warrington at Winwick Junction in 1965. It was built at Crewe Works in June 1954, but not named *Anzac* until 1959. (It was originally to be named *London & North Western*, but this never happened.) It was allocated to 7C Holyhead. It was withdrawn from 68A Carlisle Kingmoor on 8 July 1967 and scrapped at Campbell's of Airdrie four months later. Another engine that lives on as a Hornby oo scale model.

Jubilee Class 4-6-0 No. 45571 *South Africa*

A beautiful example of Stanier's taper boilered classics in the form of Jubilee 4-6-0 *South Africa* at Manchester Victoria station in 1959. It was built on 1 September 1934 at the North British Locomotive Company in Glasgow. As the London, Midland & Scottish Railway (LMS) became British Railways in 1949, it was at 24E Blackpool North shed. In 1955, it was chosen with No. 45574 *India* to pull the Royal Train to Colne. In 1963, it had 8C Speke Junction as its home, from where it was withdrawn in May 1964 and stored at Carlisle Upperby until 31 October 1964, at which time it was cut up at Connells in Coatbridge.

Dallam Shed, Warrington

Warrington Dallam shed will be mentioned frequently on these pages, but here is an atmospheric photograph of the shed in 1964 with an eclectic mix of steam engines on view. The shed was opened in 1888 by the LNWR and closed on 11 August 1968, going the way of the last of the steam engines based there. From 1831 to 1836, there had been a small engine shed and another LNWR works at Jockey Lane. A larger shed could be found near Bank Quay station from 1851 to 1888 when the new Motive Power Depot (MPD) was built opposite the old Jockey Lane Works using the building materials from there. Another shot of this MPD is featured later in the book.

Jubilee Class 4-6-0 Nos 45596 *Bahamas* and 45654 *Hood*

Two Stanier Jubilees now for the price of one: *Bahamas* and *Hood* on York depot for servicing on 4 May 1965. *Bahamas* was built on 12 March 1935 at the North British Locomotive Company in Glasgow. In 1948, it was to be found at 5A Crewe North, and its last shed was 9B Stockport Edgeley. Still going strong and preserved, it was luckier than *Hood*, which was built on 7 February 1935 at Crewe Works. In 1948, it was to be found at 14B Kentish Town, and its last shed was 26A Newton Heath from where it was withdrawn on 25 June 1966 and cut up four months later at T. W. Ward, Beighton, Sheffield.

BR Standard Class 2, 2-6-0 No. 78037

Here we see a short train with guard's van drifting into, or out of, Preston station in 1965 with the fireman relaxing during his less-than-arduous duties. The BR Standard locomotive was built at Darlington Works in November 1954 and allocated to 10B Preston. It was designed at Derby by R. A. Riddles for British Railways; its last allocation was 24C Lostock Hall, from where it was withdrawn in May 1967 and sent to Motherwell Machinery & Scrap, Inslow Works, Wishaw, where it was cut up on 30 November 1967.

Class 8P 4-6-2 No. 71000 *Duke of Gloucester*

This photograph was taken at Crewe Works in 1962 when the locomotive had been withdrawn, its chimney covered and its future unknown; now, however, we know that it was preserved. It was designed by R. A. Riddles and built on 31 May 1954 at Crewe Works as a replacement for the ex-Turbomotive engine built in 1935, converted to conventional steam engine in 1952 with No. 46202 *Princess Anne*. Then it was destroyed in its first year in the Harrow & Wealdstone train crash. The *Duke* was sent to Woodham Brothers' scrapyard in Barry to be scrapped but was one of the many engines rescued from there and into preservation in 1974.

Gresley A4 Pacific 4-6-2 No. 60019 *Bittern*

When main line steam could still be seen, there were enthusiasts' specials. After returning from one on 6 March 1966, No. 60019 can be seen at Manchester Piccadilly station. *Bittern*, like the *Duke*, was preserved and can be seen on the Mid Hants Railway. It was built on 18 December 1937 at Doncaster Works, in 1948 it was based at 52A Gateshead, and its last shed was 61B Aberdeen Ferryhill from where it was withdrawn on 5 September 1966.

Britannia Pacific Class 4-6-2 No. 70015 *Apollo*

Stockport Edgeley MPD in 1966, and we see two shots of Britannia Class engine No. 70015 *Apollo*. In the first one, it is taking on water, as the fireman stands on the tender, operating the water hose. The engine was built at Crewe Works in 1951; its last shed was 68A Carlisle Kingmoor from where it was withdrawn and sent to J. McWilliams, Shettleston and cut up in January 1968.

Britannia Pacific Class 4-6-2 No. 70015 *Apollo*

Here, the fireman climbs down and will join the driver in the cab. You can see clearly just how the hand holds were built into the windshields when the rails were taken away for safety reasons. One of the longer serving of this large class of engines, No. 70015 saw service throughout the network, being housed at many MPDs, including the first one, Camden; other London depots, Cardiff and Llandudno appear on its worksheet, as does Crewe.

Black Five 4-6-0 No. 45374

In 1967, Black Five No. 45374 is seen in rather good condition for the period – and so it should be. It has just been released from Crewe and is quite plainly ex-works as it sits in the yard at Dallam MPD in Warrington. The Stanier engine was built at Armstrong Whitworth in June 1937; in 1948, it could be found at 5A Crewe North. Its last shed was 10A Carnforth, from where it was withdrawn on 31 October 1967 and scrapped at J. McWilliams of Shettleston in May the following year.

8F Class 2-8-0 No. 48631

Our first look at one of the large class of 8F engines; this one has had the number nicely cleaned, unlike the rest of the metalwork. It is photographed passing Stockport Edgeley MPD in 1966. These engines were built as the goods version of the Stanier Black Fives, and the class was massive with 852 built between 1935 and 1946, some serving abroad during the war. This one was built at Brighton Works and, in 1961, could be found at Northwich MPD working the ICI limestone trains; it was one of the 150 that survived into 1968, being withdrawn in February of that year and broken up three months later at Cohen's of Kettering.

Royal Scot Class 4-6-0 No. 46115 *Scots Guardsman*

Scots Guardsman is photographed on an RCTS excursion at Carlisle station in 1965; the train, already preserved, is about to depart. Enjoy the memories that the engine, the driver and the platform conjure up for those old enough to remember – there will be more details on this locomotive later in the book.

9F 2-10-0 No. 92054

Here we see a mixed freight heading South towards Warrington from Winwick Junction in 1965 pulled by 9F No. 92054, designed by R. A. Riddles and built during September 1955 at Crewe Works. The first shed was 18A Toton, and its last shed was 8C Speke Junction from where it was withdrawn on 31 May 1968. It was sent to Arnott Young at Parkgate and cut up a month later at the ripe old age of thirteen years.

Black Five 4-6-0 No. 45350

It's getting very close to the end of main line steam as we see Black Five No. 45350 as it enters Manchester Victoria station in 1968 with a parcels train. This is probably one of the last photographs of this engine, as it was withdrawn after the official ending of steam on 31 August 1968. The engine was built by Armstrong Whitworth in May 1937, and allocated to 8A Edge Hill at nationalisation. In this photograph, there is a 26A shed plate, Newton Heath, but I can find details of no such allocation. It was withdrawn from 24B Rose Grove and cut up at T. W. Ward, Beighton, Sheffield on 31 December 1968.

Fairburn 2-6-4T No. 42287

A typical shed view now, in Manchester Trafford Park MPD in 1965, as a Stanier tank engine still in steam sits in the gloom. This engine was designed by Fairburn and built at Derby Works in November 1947. It was sent to 26A Newton Heath shed and the last shed from which it was withdrawn was 25A Wakefield when it was sent to Drapers, Neptune Street, Goods Yard, Hull, where it was cut up in January 1968.

Britannia Class 4-6-2 No. 70024 *Vulcan*

It is 1965 and there are still three years to go before steam is swept away, but this once-proud engine is ready for a clean. It has already lost its nameplates as it heads north towards Warrington at Moore with the evening parcels. Built in October 1951 at Crewe Works and sent to 83D Plymouth Laira, it finished its days at 68A Carlisle Kingmoor from where it was withdrawn in December 1967 and sent to T. W. Ward at Killamarsh to be cut up in April 1968.

Britannia Class 4-6-2 No. 70051 *Firth of Forth*

No. 70051 Britannia *Firth of Forth* heads south at Moore in 1966 – the previous year the engine had been involved in a tragedy near Winsford. Driver Wallace Oakes had been engulfed in flames on the footplate. He had stayed at his post and brought the train to a halt, but died a week later of his burns. He was awarded the George Cross for bravery and in 1981 an electric locomotive was named *Driver Wallace Oakes GC*. The engine was built in August 1954 at Crewe Works. It was withdrawn from Carlisle Kingmoor in December 1967 and cut up by J. McWilliams of Shettleston three months later.

Ivatt 2-6-2 tank No. 41220

Designed by Henry George Ivatt, this tank engine is seen at Stockport Edgeley in 1966. It was built at Crewe Works in October 1948 and allocated to 5A Crewe North. The last allocation was to Stockport Edgeley 9B where it was stored for a while after being fitted for push-pull. In November 1966, it was withdrawn and cut up at Cashmores of Great Bridge in June 1967.

Standard 2-6-2 tank No. 82000

9H Patricroft is the MPD and here we see one of its own engines awaiting the cutters' torch; the date is February 1967 and 82000 has been withdrawn from this depot. It was built at Swindon Works in April 1952 and allocated to 84E Tyseley. Allocated to Patricroft on 3 April 1964, it was withdrawn from here on 10 December 1966. Just two months after this photograph, in April 1967, it was cut up at Cashmores of Newport.

Crosti Boilered 9F 2-10-0 No. 92021

This not-very-successful experimental 9F heads west at Skelton Junction in 1966; it had been built in 1955 and fitted with a Crosti Boiler and pre-heater. This had been sealed off in 1959 for orthodox working. Built as part of a sub-class of ten experimental locomotives at Crewe Works, No. 92021 was allocated to 15A Wellingborough and ended its working life at 6C Birkenhead. From there, it was taken to Campbell's at Airdrie for cutting up in January 1968.

Coronation Pacific 4-6-2 No. 46237 *City of Bristol*

The driver appears to be climbing out of the window as No. 46237 *City of Bristol* leads its afternoon parcels train north past Wigan MPD in 1962. A rather mundane task for one of the greyhounds of steam traction. The Stanier-designed engine was built at Crewe Works in August 1939. On the dawning of BR in 1948, it was allocated to 1B Camden, and in 1962, it could be found at 12B Carlisle Upperby. It was withdrawn in October 1964 and two months later was scrapped at Arnott Young, Troon. This was one of the classes that was originally streamlined.

Black Five 4-6-0 No. 44884

An unusually clean Black Five heads north near Winwick Junction in 1966 with a freight train. It was built in 1945 at Crewe Works and, in 1948, allocated to 68A Carlisle Kingmoor. The last shed was 26A Newton Heath, from where it was sent for scrapping at Drapers, Neptune Street, Goods Yard, Hull, and was cut up in November 1968.

9F 2-10-0 No. 92206

This 9F heads towards Stockport in 1965, passing through Heatley & Warburton station, which closed to passengers in September 1962; it is on the LNWR line through Lymm. This line has now closed completely. The engine was only six years old, having been built at Swindon Works in May 1959, but that fact did not extend its life as its last shed was 25A Wakefield, and it was cut up at Arnott Young, Parkgate, in September 1967 at the ripe old age of eight years.

Bagnall 0-4-0 saddle tank *Trafford*

A quick dip now into a photograph of an industrial engine. In this case, one owned by Metropolitan Vickers Electrical Engineering Co. Ltd. The Bagnall saddle tank *Trafford* is seen here in 1961 in their Trafford Park Plant. These were the workhorses of many industrial plants, and steam lasted far longer there than on the mainline.

Merchant Navy Class Pacific No. 35026 *Lamport and Holt Line*

The fireman is tending to the water hose as train spotters and enthusiasts congregate to watch the engine being serviced. It is at York MPD during an enthusiasts' excursion in 1967. The excursion was for the staff of Williams Deacon's Bank (now part of RBS). The locomotive was built in December 1948 at Eastleigh Works and rebuilt in January 1957. It was withdrawn in April 1967 and cut up at Cashmores in Newport soon after.

GWR Pannier Tank No. 5775 and Ivatt 2-6-2 Tank No. 41241

Two preserved locomotives are filmed on a special in 1968 as they exit the tunnel on the Keighley & Worth Valley Railway. This is the location on the line at which a scene from *The Railway Children* was filmed; No. 5775 was the engine in the film. It was designed by Collett for the Great Western Railway and built at Swindon Works in 1929. In 1948 it could be found allocated to 87C Danygraig, and it was later withdrawn from 86G Pontypool Road on 31 July 1963. On withdrawal, it was sold to London Transport and given the number L89; it is seen in their colours here. In 1969 it was withdrawn by London Transport and sold to the K&WVR, where it still resides.

Jinty LMS 0-6-0 tank No. 47668

A small workhorse of many goods yards was the Jinty 0-6-0 tank engine, and this one is seen shunting at Bank Quay station, Warrington, in 1962. It was designed by Fowler and built in May 1931 at Horwich Works. In 1948, it was to be seen allocated to 1B Camden and after thirty-five years' hard work, it was withdrawn and delivered to Cashmores of Great Bridge where it was cut up in March 1967.

Black Five No. 45255

It is Manchester and the last year of regular steam working, 1968. Black Five No. 45255 simmers gently in the grimy surroundings of Victoria station, which would have the detritus and dirt of steam trains removed in a renovation. The engine itself was built by Armstrong Whitworth in October 1936, and on nationalisation, it was to be found allocated to 5B Crewe North. It was withdrawn from 26A Newton Heath in June 1968 and scrapped on 28 February 1969 at Drapers, Neptune Street, Goods Yard, Hull.

Ivatt 2-6-2 tanks Nos 41233 and 41202

What a brilliant photograph, taken in a packed shed in 1965. The MPD is Newton Heath, and the first of the two engines, No. 41233, was built at Crewe Works in August 1949, ending its days at Stockport Edgeley, to be cut up at Cashmores in January 1967. The second Ivatt, No. 41202, was built at Crewe Works in January 1950 and allocated to 86K Abergavenny and also ended its life at Stockport Edgeley, being cut up at T. W. Ward, Killamarsh, in March 1967.

Bagnall saddle tank

Another dip into the world of industrial locomotives, and we see a Bagnall saddle tank at work in the sidings of Metropolitan Vickers at Trafford Park in 1962. The size of the cycle shed indicates the size of this factory. It was one of the largest and most important heavy industrial facilities in Britain and the world.

Hudswell Clark tank engine

Another interesting industrial locomotive is seen here. It is a 'Long' tank Hudswell Clark locomotive built for the Manchester Ship Canal (MSC). It is seen attached to their engineers' coach, which at the time was acting as the pay coach for its employees along the length of the canal. It is seen at Latchford locks, with the Richmond Gas Stove Co. in the background, around 1962. The MSC Railway was not nationalised and became the largest private railway system in Britain. It was built to service the company's docks. At its peak, it employed some 800 employees, with 75 locomotives, over 2,000 wagons and 200 miles of track. The line was closed to all traffic in 1978.

GWR Pannier Tank No. 5775 and Ivatt 2-6-2 Tank No. 41241

Having looked on a previous page at the pannier tank engine at the K&WVR, let's now look at the 2-6-2. No. 41241 is a 2MT A engine, designed by Ivatt and built at Crewe Works in September 1949. Its last allocation was 10G Skipton, and it went eventually to the K&WVR for preservation. It is currently under heavy repair and will be back on the lines sometime in 2018.

Black Five No. 45033 with new D277

This excellent photograph was taken at Derby station in 1960 (yes, I know it is slightly south, but the image is, you will agree, well worth it) as Black Five No. 45033 pulled the next generation of motive power, the new D277. The Black Five, designed by Stanier, was built at the Vulcan Foundry in Newton-le-Willows in September 1934. This workshop was building locomotives from the very early days of the railways worldwide, and it closed in 2002; its products can still be found around the world. The last shed allocation for No. 45033 was 5B Crewe South from where it was withdrawn in December 1966. It was cut up at Drapers, Neptune Street, Goods Yard, Hull, in September 1967.

The new diesel D277 was built at the same works as the Black Five and introduced in May 1960, although by then the works had the initials EE/VF (English Electric/Vulcan Foundry). It was allocated to 50A York and received its TOPS (Total Operations Processing System) No. 40077 in March 1974. It was withdrawn from Longsight MPD in June 1983 and cut up at Doncaster Works in April 1984.

Jubilee Class 4-6-0 No. 45600 *Bermuda*

Jubilee No. 45600 *Bermuda* is seen hauling its train south out of Warrington Bank Quay station in 1964. Built in February 1935, it was allocated to 5A Crewe North in 1948. Its last shed was 26A Newton Heath, from where it was withdrawn on 18 December 1965 for delivery to Cashmores of Great Bridge, where it was cut up on 30 April 1966.

Crosti-boilered 9F 2-10-0 No. 92022

Trundling along the LNWR line to Stockport, we see one of the small sub-classes of Crosti-boilered 9Fs as it leads a train of coal empties near Thelwall in 1965. Designed by R. A. Riddles, like the rest of the class, it was built at Crewe Works in May 1955 and allocated to 15A Wellingborough. It was withdrawn from 6C Birkenhead in November 1967 and cut up at Campbell's of Airdrie four months later.

Thomson B1 4-6-0 No. 61319

Photographed at York in 1965 is this Thompson-designed B1 as it sits in front of a diesel in a bleak and barren railway yard. The engine was built by the North British Locomotive Co. in Glasgow in May 1948 and allocated to 54C Borough Gardens, a sub shed of Gateshead MPD. Its last shed was 50A North York, from where it was withdrawn in December 1966. It was cut up exactly two months later at Drapers, Neptune Street Goods Yard, Hull.

Royal Scot Class 4-6-0 No. 46102 *Black Watch*

1962 and it is back to Dallam shed in Warrington, where we find one of the most elusive engines during my train spotting days: No. 46102 *Black Watch*, named after one of the Scottish regiments in the First World War, which the Germans nicknamed 'The Ladies from Hell' due to their bravery and practice of going over the top in their kilts. This engine, though, named as a tribute to those brave men, was built in September 1927 at the North British Locomotive Works in Glasgow, and on nationalisation in 1948, it was allocated to 66A Polmadie. Its final shed from which it was withdrawn in December 1962 was 67A Corkerhill. It was cut up in May 1964 at J. McWilliams, Shettleston. The photograph shows it very close to withdrawal, and it seems to be in remarkably good condition. Another locomotive that has joined the oo gauge club, having been made by Hornby, No. R2628.

Dallam shed 1965

I don't think that you can get enough of shed views during the days of steam – and here is another of Dallam shed, filled with all classes of steam engines. The engine in the foreground, with plenty of steam to spare, is now devoid of a name on the windshields, but it is Britannia No. 70010 *Owen Glendower*. This engine was built at Crewe Works on 5 May 1951 and allocated to 32A Norwich Thorpe. Its last shed was 68A Carlisle Kingmoor, from where it was withdrawn in September 1967 and sent to J. McWilliams of Shettleston, where it was cut up on 17 January 1968.

Royal Scot 4-6-0 No. 46115 *Scots Guardsman*

As we look up at the front of No. 46115 *Scots Guardsman*, enthusiasts tick it off in their Ian Allan *ABC*s. The train is preparing to leave Crewe station on 13 February 1965 on an enthusiasts' excursion, in this case, The Royal Scot Commemorative Tour. The engine was built at the North British Locomotive in Glasgow in October 1927. In 1948, it was allocated to 5A Crewe North, and its last shed was 68A Carlisle Kingmoor from where it was withdrawn on 1 January 1966.

No. 46115 *Scots Guardsman*

On the same Royal Scot Commemorative Tour, we see *Scots Guardsman* as it arrives at Carlisle on 13 February 1965. The yellow stripe on the cab side means that, at this time, it was not allowed to work south beyond Crewe. It is now preserved and licensed for main line work until 2018. So there are plenty more enthusiasts' specials for this iconic engine.

Ex-Works WD/8 2-8-0 No. 90722

Photographed at the head of a freight at Trafford Park, Manchester, in 1964, is an engine from the war years – well, the end of those horrendous years anyway. It was built at the Vulcan Foundry in April 1945 for the War Department with the number 79298. In September 1949, it was transferred to BR and given the number 90722. In 1957, it was allocated to 55E Normanton and withdrawn in June 1967. It was scrapped at Arnott Young, Parkgate, in November of that year.

8F 2-8-0 No. 48045

Another engine from the massive class of 8F locomotives, some of which gave excellent service during the last war: in this case, No. 48045 is on the Warrington to Stockport line near Thelwall in 1962 with a train of empty coal wagons. This was one of those engines built at the Vulcan Foundry in September 1936, requisitioned by the War Department in 1941 and sent to Persia. It was returned in December 1944 and reallocated to the LMS for work in Britain. It was withdrawn and scrapped in August 1968 at T. W. Ward at Killamarsh.

9F 2-10-0 No. 92133

Here we find 9F No. 92133 on an Ellesmere Port tank train, seen at Thelwall in 1965. Built in June 1957 at Crewe Works and allocated to 21A Saltley, its last shed from which it was withdrawn in July 1967 was 6C Birkenhead, almost exactly ten years from its date of building. It was cut up at T. J. Thompson & Sons, Stockton, in January 1968.

Ivatt 2-6-2T No. 41222

An action shot now of Ivatt 2-6-2 No. 41222 scuttling through Carlisle station in 1965. It was built in October 1948 at Crewe Works and allocated to 5A Crewe North. It was later fitted with push-pull and used on the Newport Pagnell branch until it closed in 1964. The engine was withdrawn from its final shed 68A Carlisle Kingmoor in December 1966 from where it was taken to J. McWilliams in Shettleston to be cut up in September 1967.

Black Five 4-6-0 and 9F 2-10-0

Here we see a double-headed heavy coal train travelling towards Warrington at Thelwall in 1963, no numbers here but an unusual coupling for a double header. It gives us a good atmospheric shot of two hard-working steam engines.

Jinty 0-6-0T No. 47350

In Dallam shed at Warrington in 1962, Jinty 0-6-0 No. 47350 pokes its nose out of the shed building as an engine is being flashed up next to it. Designed by Fowler and built in 1926 at the North British Locomotive Works in Glasgow, the Jinty could be found at 1D Devon's Road shed in 1948. It was withdrawn in December 1965 and delivered to the Central Wagon Company, Ince, Wigan, to be cut up in January 1966.

Stanier 2-6-0 No. 42960

Not one of the most common of William Stanier's designs, No. 42960 heads south near Wigan with a local train in 1963. The class consisted of forty locomotives and was introduced in 1933. Commonly known as Moguls, they were some of Stanier's first designs after he joined Crewe from the Great Western Railway (GWR) (work had already started on the class at Horwich Works). This engine was built in December 1933 at Crewe Works. Its last shed was 13C Heaton Mersey, from where it was withdrawn in January 1966 and delivered to T. W. Ward at Killamarsh, where it was cut up three months later.

Britannia Class 4-6-2 No. 70017 *Arrow*

A first-class action shot now of a powerful steam engine at work as No. 70017 *Arrow* heads north towards Warrington at Moore in 1964. Built at Crewe Works in June 1951, this engine was involved in a collision at St Nicholas, Carlisle. It was hauling empty passenger carriages when it collided with the rear of a goods train in July 1966 and was derailed. Damage was light but it was decided that it was uneconomic to repair. Accordingly, it was withdrawn from 68A Carlisle Kingmoor in October 1966 and cut up at Cashmores, Newport, in January 1967.

No. 46256 *Sir William A. Stanier FRS* and English Electric Class 82 with Diesel

Here we are in Crewe station with a mix of steam, electric and diesel; the year is around 1963, and we look at *Sir William A. Stanier* later in the book. As for the electric loco, it is E3055, the last of the Class 82s to be built and was quite new. It was built by Beyer Peacock and introduced in April 1962. There is no TOPS number as this locomotive was destroyed in a fire at Maw Green, Crewe, in 1966 and scrapped at Crewe Works in August 1970. (The first of the class built, E3046, was also destroyed by fire but in 1971.)

Rebuilt Patriot Class 4-6-0 No. 45531 *Sir Frederick Harrison*

Another visit to Warrington Dallam shed in 1963 where we find one of the rebuilt Patriot class engines, *Sir Frederick Harrison*. Designed by Henry Fowler, it was named after Sir Frederick Harrison, a senior railway manager who rose through the ranks. The engine was built in April 1933 at Crewe Works and was rebuilt in 1946 by H. G. Ivatt with a taper boiler and resembling the Royal Scot Class. On nationalisation, it could be found at 3B Bushbury, and its last shed was 68A Carlisle Kingmoor from where it was withdrawn during October 1965 and cut up at Campbell's of Airdrie during the following January. Only eighteen engines of the class were rebuilt and No. 45531 was one of the last to be withdrawn; none were preserved.

Jinty 0-6-0T No. 47357

Another Jinty, this time hidden away at the back of Trafford Park shed in 1965, and quite a lucky Jinty, this one, as it is still with us. It was designed by Fowler and built in 1926 at the North British Locomotive Works in Glasgow. In 1948, it could be found allocated to 1A Willesden. In December 1966, it was withdrawn and, in 1967, sold to Woodham Brothers at Barry. Rescued in 1970 by the Midland Railway and after service at Butterley, at the time of writing, it is undergoing a major overhaul.

Jubilee Class 4-6-0 No. 45593 *Kolhapur*

It is 1964 and seen in the Leeds Holbeck shed is No. 45593 *Kolhapur*. Who would have thought at the time that this dirty, scruffy engine would one day be brought back to life in the form of a vibrantly painted preserved Jubilee. It was built in December 1934 at the North British Locomotive Works in Glasgow and, in 1949, could be found allocated to 9A Longsight. Its last shed was 20A Leeds Holbeck, and it was withdrawn from there in October 1967. In October 1968, it was purchased by Clun Castle Ltd. At the time of writing, it is temporarily out of service.

Gresley B1 4-6-0 No. 61131

Over to 56A Wakefield shed in 1964, where we find No. 61131 looking in quite good condition in view of the nearing of the end of steam. The engine was designed by Nigel Gresley/Edward Thompson and built at the North British Locomotive Works in Glasgow in February 1947. In 1949, it was allocated to 38E Woodford Halse, and its last shed was 25A Wakefield from where it was withdrawn in December 1966. Two months later, it was cut up at Drapers, Neptune Street, Goods Yard, Hull.

Royal Scot 7P 4-6-0 No. 46128 *The Lovat Scouts*

Here we see a rather grubby Royal Scot, travelling southbound with a goods train as it passes through Warrington Bank Quay station in 1965. The name plates have been removed for safe keeping. The engine is a Fowler/Stanier design, built during September 1927 at the North British Locomotive Co. in Glasgow. In 1948 it could be found allocated to 12A Carlisle Upperby, while its last shed was 68A Carlisle Kingmoor, from where it was withdrawn in May 1965, shortly after the photograph was taken. It was cut up two months later at Motherwell Machinery and Scrap, Inslow Works, Wishaw.

LNER B1 Class 4-6-0 No. 61315

Manchester Central station in 1961: in among the steam we have a B1 class LNER engine. It was built at the North British Locomotive Works in Glasgow during April 1948, having been designed by Edward Thompson for the LNER. Its first allocation upon nationalisation was 39A Gorton, while its last shed was 40E Langwith Junction. It was withdrawn on 10 February 1966; however, it then acquired the number 32 as it enjoyed further service heating coaches at Canklow locomotive depot at Rotherham. In October 1968 it was cut up at Hesslewoods of Attercliffe.

8F 2-8-0 No. 48715

It is 1964 and 8F No. 48715 heads north near Warrington with a mixed goods. It was built at Brighton Works in 1944, and on nationalisation, it was allocated to 24B Rose Grove. It spent time at various sheds in the North West, and in May 1968, it returned to Rose Grove from where it was withdrawn on the last month of main line steam working, August 1968, and cut up at T. W. Ward, Beighton, Sheffield, in December 1968.

8F 2-8-0 No. 48017

It is 1965, and 8F No. 48017 heads north towards Warrington at Moore signal box. The engine was built at Crewe Works in January 1937, and its first shed upon nationalisation was 19A Sheffield Grimesthorpe. It was withdrawn from 8A Edge Hill in October 1967 and cut up in July 1968.

Black Five 4-6-0 No. 44935

Light engine, Black Five No. 44935 is seen passing through Bank Quay station at Warrington in 1962 as the driver gives Phil a big smile. The engine was built in October 1946 and allocated to 8A Edge Hill. Its last shed was Warrington Dallam, and it was withdrawn from there in October 1966 and cut up at Cashmore's of Great Bridge in April 1967.

Britannia Class 4-6-2 No. 70014 *Iron Duke*

Preston station is the location of *Iron Duke* as it awaits the 'right away' signal, and the driver takes the opportunity to check his locomotive. The engine is in a very good condition for 1966, and this is possibly down to enthusiasts with their oily cloths. The engine was built at Crewe Works in June 1951 to the design of R. A. Riddles, and it was allocated to 32A Norwich Thorpe. Its last shed was 68A Carlisle Kingmoor, from where it was withdrawn in December 1967 and scrapped at T. W. Ward at Killamarsh in March 1968.

Jubilee No. 45655 *Keith*

Longsight loco depot, Manchester, in 1962 where we find a selection of motive power starting with Jubilee *Keith*. The engine was built in December 1934 at Derby Works, and it was withdrawn from 8B Warrington Dallam in April 1965 and cut up at R. S. Hayes, Tremains Yard, Bridgend, eight months later. EE type diesel D227, later No. 40077, was introduced in May 1960 and scrapped in April 1984. There is also an unknown LNER B1.

Rebuilt Patriot Class 4-6-0 7P No. 45527 *Southport*

Photographed at speed and close up on the southbound bank out of Warrington is rebuilt Patriot class engine *Southport*. It was built at Derby Works in March 1933 to a design by Henry Fowler and rebuilt in 1946 to a design by George Ivatt with a large taper boiler, a double chimney and advanced cylinders. In 1948, it could be found allocated to 8A Edge Hill, and after gracing many sheds, it was withdrawn from Carlisle Kingmoor in September 1964 and cut up at Arnott Young in Troon in April 1965.

Jubilees Nos 45741 *Leinster* and 45563 *Australia*

Still on Warrington Dallam shed in 1963, we find two Jubilees, first of which is No. 45741 *Leinster*. It was built in December 1936 at Crewe Works and withdrawn from 68A Carlisle Kingmoor in February 1964. It was cut up at Crewe Works two months later. The other engine, No. 45563 *Australia*, was built in August 1934 at the North British Locomotive Works in Glasgow. It was withdrawn from this shed in November 1965 and cut up at Cashmores of Great Bridge in April 1966.

Royal Scot Class 4-6-0 No. 46155 *The Lancer*

The Lancer, with the yellow stripe to show that it is not allowed south of Crewe, is seen under the wires. In this case, it heads off for servicing from Crewe station to Crewe North MPD in 1964. The engine was built in July 1930 at Derby Works, and on nationalisation, it was allocated to 5A Crewe North. Its last shed from where it was withdrawn was 68A Carlisle Kingmoor in December 1964, being cut up at Arnott Young in Troon in February 1965. Just two Royal Scot engines went into preservation, *Royal Scot* and *Scots Guardsman*.

Jubilee 4-6-0 No. 45666 *Cornwallis*

Hidden away in the dark recesses of Newton Heath MPD in 1964 is a once-powerful Jubilee, soon to face the cutters' torch. Built at Crewe Works during November 1935, it was allocated to 8A Edge Hill, while its last shed was 8B Warrington Dallam, from where it was withdrawn on 17 April 1965 and cut up at RS Hayes/Birds, Tremains Yard, Bridgend, on 31 August 1965.

2-6-0 No. 78008

The driver looks out disconsolately as a grubby No. 78008 brings a parcels train into Manchester Exchange in 1964. The engine, designed by R. A. Riddles, was built in March 1953 at Darlington Works. It was withdrawn from 84B Oxley in October 1966 and scrapped at Cashmore's of Great Bridge in January 1967.

Britannia Class 4-6-2 No. 70025 *Western Star*

How sad the locomotives were getting as 1968 approached. Here we see No. 70025 *Western Star* hauling a freight through Preston station in 1966. The name plates have gone and been replaced with a handwritten name and number. Built in September 1952 and allocated to Cardiff Canton, the last shed was 68A Carlisle Kingmoor, from where it was withdrawn in December 1967 and cut up at Campbell's of Airdrie the following month.

Standard Class 4MT 2-6-0 No. 76079

Seen near Winwick Junction, No. 76079 heads north in 1967 and is in excellent condition, as befits an engine that is to be preserved. It was built at Horwich Works in February 1957 and then allocated to 10D Bolton Plodder Lane. Its last shed was 10A Wigan Springs Branch, from where it was withdrawn in December 1967. It was purchased by Ian Riley Engineering, and on 27 August 2009, it was sold to the North Yorkshire Moors Railway where it can now be found back on the rails and in an even better condition than is seen here.

B1 Class 4-6-0 No. 61014

A nice photograph of a rather grubby B1 in the form of No. 61014 at Stockport Edgeley in 1964. Designed by Thompson and built in December 1946 at Darlington Works, its first allocation was to 52A Gateshead. In the photograph, the shed plate shows 56F Low Moor, but the last shed from which the engine was withdrawn was 52F North Blyth, the date being December 1966; from there it was taken to Hughes Bolckow, Battleship Wharf, North Blyth, and cut up.

Standard 4MT 4-6-0 No. 75032

This sad-looking Riddles-designed locomotive is seen at Preston in 1966 with a non-standard number plate and a missing shed plate. A perfect example of steam during the period, it was built at Swindon Works in June 1953 and allocated as a very attractive engine to 4A Bletchley. It had a busy life, being constantly reallocated to locations mainly around the North; its last shed was 11A Carnforth, from where it was withdrawn on 29 February 1968. It was cut up at T. W. Ward, Beighton, Sheffield, three months later.

Warrington Dallam shed in 1965

Another typical steam shed view as we look at Dallam MPD in Warrington with two engines plainly visible. Designed by R. A. Riddles, 9F locomotive 2-10-0 No. 92055 was built at Crewe Works during September 1955 and allocated to 18A Toton MPD. It was withdrawn from 8C Speke Junction on 31 December 1967 and scrapped four months later at T. W. Ward, Killamarsh. The second engine in the foreground is Black Five 4-6-0 No. 45448. Built at Armstrong Whitworth in December 1937, at nationalisation in 1948 it could be found at 2A Rugby. The last shed was 13C Heaton Mersey, from where it was withdrawn on 31 August 1967 and scrapped at T. W. Ward, Beighton, Sheffield, on 31 January 1968.

Royal Scot Class 4-6-0 No. 46115 *Scots Guardsman*

Another clear photograph of No. 46115 *Scots Guardsman*, and it is in a very good condition on 13 February 1965 when it can be seen at Carlisle station on a special. The condition may have influenced its later purchase as it was withdrawn in January 1966 from Carlisle Kingmoor. In August of that year, it was taken to the Keighley & Worth Valley Railway to begin life again. In 2008, it was purchased by the West Coast Railway where it was returned to main line running and can be seen on classic trains across Britain. In 2012, the Olympic Torch was to be carried from York to Shildon by A3 No. 60103 *Flying Scotsman*, but due to her being unavailable, the torch was carried by *Scots Guardsman*, one of only two of these attractive locomotives that were preserved.

Britannia Class 4-6-2 No. 70053 *Moray Firth*

It is Crewe station in 1962, and *Moray Firth* shares a bay with a local electric railcar. The 4-6-2 was built at Crewe Works in September 1954 and allocated to 66A Polmadie. Its last shed was 68A Carlisle Kingmoor, from where it was withdrawn in April 1967 and scrapped in September the same year by J. McWilliams, Shettleston. The engine's handrails have been replaced with hand grips on the windshields that still display the name plates.

Jinty 0-6-0 tank No. 47326

Back to the mundane workhorses now in the form of a ubiquitous Jinty, seen here on station pilot duty at Carlisle in September 1965 as it blows off steam. This Fowler engine was built in July 1926 at the North British Locomotive Works in Glasgow. In 1948, it could be found at 12A Carlisle Upperby, and it was withdrawn in December 1966. It was scrapped at J. McWilliams, Shettleston, in September 1967.

Jubilee Class 4-6-0 No. 45604 *Ceylon*

Seen alongside the platform at Warrington Bank Quay station in 1962, waiting for the passengers to enter and leave the train. The Stanier Jubilee was built at the North British Locomotive Works in Glasgow in March 1935 and in 1949 was found at 20A Leeds Holbeck. The last shed that it was allocated to was 26A Newton Heath, from where it was withdrawn in July 1965 and cut up at Cashmore's of Great Bridge in October the same year.

Black Five 4-6-0 No. 45128

This is at Warrington Bank Quay station as No. 45128 restarts a parcels train in 1962 with the large soap factory (Crosfield's) in the background. It was built in May 1935 at Armstrong Whitworth and in 1948 was allocated to 5B Crewe South. Its last shed was 10A Wigan Springs Branch and, on 30 September 1966, it was withdrawn. On 3 March 1967, it was cut up at Cashmore's of Great Bridge.

Jubilee Class 4-6-0 No. 45552 *Silver Jubilee*

Oh how the mighty fall – here, we see a dirty, scruffy 4-6-0 No. 45552 *Silver Jubilee* as it heads a southbound short train at Moore in 1966. This famous engine was built at Crewe Works in June 1934 as No. 5552. The following year, in April, it swapped identities with No. 5642, which had been built in December 1935 (No. 5642 was later named *Boscawen*). *Silver Jubilee* was the first of what came to be known as the Jubilee Class. It was given special treatment. The Jubilees were painted in 'crimson lake' (red) but *Silver Jubilee* was repainted in all-over black with silver lining. It was given specially cast chrome numbers and named *Silver Jubilee*; this was all to mark the silver jubilee of King George V. It remained like this until its first allocation at nationalisation, which was 9A Longsight, at which time it was renumbered 45552. Its last shed was Crewe North; it was withdrawn on 26 September 1964 and cut up at Cashmore's of Great Bridge on 31 January 1965.

Whatever the condition of the engine at withdrawal, the person making the decision to scrap such an iconic engine did no one any favours. Since the demise of the engine, other preserved engines have been disguised to look like it; for instance, No. 45593 *Kolhapur* was painted in the original livery to mark the silver jubilee of the preserved Great Central Railway during 2003.

8F 2-8-0 No. 48668

No. 48668 is seen on a heavy coal train near Copy Pit in the early 1960s. The engine was built in 1944 at Eastleigh Locomotive Works and was withdrawn in September 1965 from 16G Westhouses. In December 1965, it was cut up at T. W. Ward, Beighton, Sheffield.

Standard Class 5MT 4-6-0 No. 73131

This Class 5MT engine is seen heading towards Warrington at Winwick Junction in 1962. Designed by R. A. Riddles and fitted with Caprotti valve gear and a BR tender, it was built at Derby Works in September 1956. It was first allocated to 84G Shrewsbury, and its last shed was 10C Patricroft, from where it was withdrawn in January 1968. It was cut up at Cashmore's of Newport four months later. These engines were the next generation of the large class of Stanier Black Fives, more efficient, faster and easier to maintain.

Black Five 4-6-0 No. 45421
Now a look at one of the ubiquitous Black Five engines as it heads south at Winwick Junction towards Warrington in 1965. Some wag has chalked 'Wigan for the cup' on the smoke box. This one was built at Armstrong Whitworth in October 1937. The massive Armstrong Whitworth Company, based at Newcastle upon Tyne, built 327 Black Fives at their factory in Scotswood Road between 1935 and 1937, as well as many locomotives for worldwide use. Its last shed was 24C Lostock Hall, from where it was withdrawn on 29 February 1968 and scrapped four months later at T. W. Ward, Beighton, Sheffield.

Black Five 4-6-0 No. 45134
Another Black Five, this time southbound near Preston in 1967. The year was the last full year before the end of steam traction altogether, and the engine is suitably dirty to reflect this. It was built in May 1935 by Armstrong Whitworth and in 1948 it could be found at 5B Crewe South. The last shed that it was allocated to was 11A Carnforth and from there it was withdrawn on 31 August 1968, the last month of mainline steam. In January 1969, it was broken up at Cohen's of Kettering.

Merchant Navy Pacific No. 35028 *Clan Line*

This beautiful engine is seen on an excursion close to Mobberley in Cheshire on an unknown date. It will be well after the end of steam, as the engine is one of the most famous to have been preserved and used on specials on the main line. It will not be seen for a while though, as in 2015 it went into Crewe Works for a full overhaul. Its last journey was from London Victoria to Crewe, then to Chester where it was turned and serviced before returning to Crewe Works. Its place on preserved steam traction will be taken by the brand new Peppercorn A1 4-6-2 No. 60163 *Tornado*, completed in 2008.

Standard 5MT 4-6-0

This unidentified engine is included in the book as the photograph is so atmospheric. The Standard 5MT heads north out of Warrington past the old Central line that goes over the WCML. It is 1962, and the engine is pulling a small goods train with a selection of different rolling stock. Just enjoy this peep into the days of steam as the engine sends up a powerful blast of smoke, and the guard will be sitting in his guard's van doing a job that would not be there for long.

Black Five 4-6-0 No. 45018

This Stanier Black Five with a small snow plough and a Carlisle Kingmoor (12A) shed plate sits in its own fog of steam. Designed by Stanier as a jack of all trades locomotive, the Black Fives could be found across the country on just about every form of work from passenger to goods and, towards the end, station pilots and the like. The engine was built at Crewe Works in May 1935 and in 1949 was at 66B Motherwell. Its last shed was 12A Carlisle Kingmoor, from where it was withdrawn in December 1966. Not sent directly to the cutter's torch, it was sent to Eastfield Shed in Glasgow to be used as a stationary boiler. It was later scrapped at Drapers, Neptune Street, Goods Yard, Hull.

Jubilee Class 4-6-0 No. 45647 *Sturdee*

Here we see an excellent photograph of one of the best-looking engines that Stanier designed, in this case Jubilee 4-6-0 *Sturdee*, on the old LNWR line near Thelwall in 1963. The shed plate shows it to be allocated to 55C Farnley, a sub-shed of its last allocation, 20A Leeds Holbeck. The engine was built in January 1935 and could be found at 5A Crewe North in 1948, and its last shed was the aforementioned Leeds Holbeck, from where it was withdrawn in April 1967 and sent to Cashmore's of Great Bridge where it was cut up in September 1967.

Black Five 4-6-0 No. 45104

Another of the ubiquitous Stanier Black Fives as it comes off the LNWR line at Arpley, Warrington, and heads up towards Moore in 1965. With plenty of coal on the fire, the fireman can relax and look out at the countryside and the photographer. Built in May 1935 at the Vulcan Foundry in Newton-le-Willows, it was allocated to 26B Agecroft in 1949, and its last shed was 26C Bolton when it was withdrawn in June 1968 and sent to Cohen's of Kettering, where it was broken up in October the same year.

GWR 4-6-0s, going for scrap

Here we have sixteen once-powerful engines, built for the Great Western Railway, being towed by a 5MT locomotive at Winwick Junction, near Warrington, in 1963. Their numbers are not known but they are being towed behind a Black Five. These sights were commonplace as August 1968 approached. In some cases, the towing locomotive was also heading for the scrap yard and its own demise.

Britannia Class 4-6-2 No. 70014 *Iron Duke*

Another look at this Britannia class engine as it awaits the 'right away' in Preston station with a parcels train for the north in 1966. Although it has already lost its name plates, it is in a remarkably good condition and has plenty of steam to spare. The Black Five up ahead, also with a parcels train, has not fared quite so well and is showing the effects of an engine drawing near to the fateful day in August 1968 when regular mainline steam was ended.

A Crewe Works Fowler 0-6-0s Shunter

No number here in this view of a jack-of-all-trades in the railway sheds and yards. This one is a really rough engine, even for these end of steam days. Designed by Henry Fowler for the LMS and nicknamed, among other things, 'Duck Sixes' because of their wheel arrangement, all of them were withdrawn between 1959 and 1966, with just three being preserved.

8F 2-8-0 No. 48254

Northwich shed, where I have many happy memories of the inside of this small MPD with its many memorable smells. (It was near our school and easily bunked!) The year is 1962 and the 8F is on its own turf, being allocated to 8E Northwich to cover the limestone hopper trains from the Buxton mines to the ICI works. In this photograph, the engine is paired with an old Fowler tender. This engine was built from 1940 to 1942 at the North British Locomotive Works in Glasgow for the War Department with the number 70378. It was then returned from WD stock in December 1949 for use on BR and renumbered. It was withdrawn from 18B Westhouses in September 1966 and scrapped in November of the same year at Cashmore's of Great Bridge.

Black Five 4-6-0 No. 45282

It is a very wet day in 1963, but this has not deterred the sole train spotter on Patricroft station as Black Five No. 45282 trundles through with a passenger train for Manchester. There are five years yet to August 1968, but the Black Five is in a truly scruffy state. The engine was built in November 1936 by Armstrong Whitworth and in 1948 it could be found at 2C Warwick shed. In May 1968 it was at 8A Edge Hill shed when it was withdrawn and stored at Heaton Mersey until October, when it was scrapped by T. W. Ward at Killamarsh.

Black Five 4-6-0 No. 45405

An atmospheric photograph of working steam as Black Five No. 45405 hauls a train of coal empties at Glazebrook in 1962. The engine was built in September 1937 by Armstrong Whitworth, and in 1948, it was allocated to 3B Bushbury. It was withdrawn from 5D Stoke in August 1967 and cut up at J. Buttigiegs at Newport five months later.

Black Five 4-6-0

A scene that I witnessed even earlier than this as a proud steam engine hauled one of the next generation of locomotives on the railways. In this case, an unknown and filthy Black Five hauls a new electric loco, No. E3155, towards Crewe in 1966. The location is south of Winwick Junction, heading towards Warrington. The electric locomotive is a BR/EE 25Kv Bo-Bo Class 86 that was built at the Vulcan Foundry and was introduced in April 1966. It later had the TOPS No. 86234, and in December 1980 it was named *J. B. Priestley OM*.

B1 4-6-0 No. 61281

It is Doncaster in 1963 as the driver or fireman oils B1 No. 61281, and it looks to be in line for taking on coal with a 9F 2-10-0 in front of it. It is only 1963, but the engine looks to be in need of some TLC. It was designed by Edward Thompson and built at the North British Locomotive Works in Glasgow in January 1948 and allocated to 40A Lincoln. Its last shed was 38A Colwick, from where it was withdrawn in February 1966 and cut up three months later at Birds of Long Marston.

5MT 4-6-0 No. 45182 and Jubilee (on the right) No. 45580 *Burma*

No. 45182 thunders past Winwick Quay near Warrington with a southbound passenger train in 1963. Meanwhile, Jubilee *Burma* potters light engine on the other side of the box. The Stanier-designed 5MT or Black Five was built in September 1935 by Armstrong Whitworth and, in 1948, it could be found at 10C Patricroft. Its last shed was 11B Barrow, from where it was withdrawn in March 1966 and broken up at the Arnott Young scrapyard eight months later.

Flying Scotsman No. 60103 (LNER 4472)

Here is an example of the interest that there was in main line steam even before the mass culling of steam engines. On 18 September 1965, the preserved *Flying Scotsman* arrives at Cheadle Heath on an LCGB (Locomotive Club of Great Britain) excursion. The engine was built at Doncaster Works in February 1923, having been designed by Nigel Gresley. Its first BR shed was 36A Doncaster, and it was withdrawn in January 1963 from 34A King's Cross. In 1924, the engine was displayed at the British Empire Exhibition, and it was here that the locomotive became famous, with the addition of a special tender with a corridor to the train, enabling the crew to change without stopping; it was the first engine to pull a train non-stop from London to Edinburgh. In 1934, it achieved 100 mph on a test run. When withdrawn, it was purchased by Alan Pegler and given a complete overhaul. In 1969, it went on tour to the USA where it was stranded for a while due to Alan Pegler going into bankruptcy. William McAlpine put together a rescue plan, and the engine toured Australia before returning to continue with its duties on Britain's railways, but with a number of new owners and several ups and downs.

In 2004, the National Railway Museum started a campaign to save what had become a national treasure and the oldest steam locomotive still on the main line. With grants from the National Heritage Memorial Fund and the Heritage Lottery Fund, not to mention massive support from the general public, the engine is once again in tip-top condition. At the time of writing, Network Rail has overturned its decision to restrict steam on the main line in Scotland, and *Flying Scotsman* will be taking to the tracks of Fife and the Borders on a Steam Special.

Coronation Class 4-6-2 No. 46256 *Sir William A. Stanier FRS*

What a brilliant photograph, taken at Crewe station on 24 September 1964, of Coronation Class *Sir William A. Stanier FRS*. The engine crew look out from the footplate, and it bears the yellow line, indicating that it cannot travel south of Crewe under the wires. This beautiful engine was built at Crewe Works in December 1947 to the design of Sir William, when H. G. Ivatt had taken over from him as Chief Mechanical Engineer (CME). Ivatt made some changes, including roller bearings and other minor changes. This was one of the last two of the classes to be built and was named as a tribute to Sir William, who had been the designer of so many excellent engines running on Britain's railways. It was allocated to 5A Crewe North, from where it was withdrawn in October 1964. Then, two months later, in what seems like a crime nowadays, it was cut up at Cashmores of Great Bridge.

Jubilee Class 4-6-0 No. 45574 *India*

No. 45574 Jubilee *India* heads north at Leyland in 1963 with a short passenger train. The locomotive was designed by William Stanier and built at the North British Locomotive Co. in Glasgow. The date of building was 29 September 1934 and on nationalisation it could be found at 28A Blackpool Central. Its last allocation was 20A Leeds Holbeck, from where it was withdrawn on 31 March 1966. On 31 August 1968 it was cut up at Drapers, Neptune Street Goods Yard, Hull.

5MT No. 45292

It's 1963 and Black Five No. 45292 heads north at Leyland with a short passenger train. It left the builders, Armstrong Whitworth, in December 1936 and in 1948 it could be found at 84G Shrewsbury. Its last shed was 6C Birkenhead, from where it was withdrawn on 30 November 1967 and cut up at Cashmores in Great Bridge in March 1967. This is another engine that can be found as a Hornby oo gauge model.

Castle Class 4-6-0 No. 7029 *Clun Castle*

Another engine during the days of steam that went on to be preserved, *Clun Castle* is seen here on 4 March 1967 near Crewe with an Ian Allan special, The Zulu. The engine was designed by Charles Collett, built at Swindon Works in May 1950 and allocated to 83A Newton Abbot. It was part of a large class of 171 locomotives, of which *Clun Castle* was the last to be withdrawn, in December 1965 from 85B Gloucester Horton Road. It was bought for its scrap value of £2,400 in 1966; its later home was the Tyseley TMD/Locomotive Works. It has had a busy life in the preserved sector and is at the time of writing undergoing an overhaul and should be returning to traffic this year. The name on the photograph, Ian Allan, The Zulu, was one of a number of specials with the code 1X83, and this one ran from Banbury to Chester General via Birmingham Snow Hill, Wolverhampton Low Level and Shrewsbury and back from Chester General to Birmingham Snow Hill via Shrewsbury and Wolverhampton Low Level.

Black Five 4-6-0 No. 45411 and Mogul 2-6-0 No. 46418

A rather dirty and unkempt Newton Heath shed in 1967 with Black Five No. 45411 in the foreground. The Stanier engine was built in September 1937 by Armstrong Whitworth and in 1948 could be found at 10C Patricroft. It was withdrawn from Newton Heath shed in June 1968 and scrapped at Drapers, Neptune Street, Goods Yard, Hull, three months later. Mogul No. 46418 was designed by George Ivatt and built at Crewe Works in March 1947. In 1949, it was allocated to this shed and was withdrawn from here in January 1967 and cut up at Cashmore's in September 1967. Also in the yard is a Cowans and Sheldon breakdown crane.

Black Five No. 45259

This is Warrington Bank Quay sidings in 1967 as a breakdown crane sets off to relieve some mishap somewhere on the network. The engine in charge is a Stanier Black Five No. 45259; this engine left the builders, Armstrong Whitworth, in October 1936 and in 1948 could be found at 10C Patricroft. It was withdrawn from its last shed, 68A Carlisle Kingmoor, in December 1967 and cut up at T. W. Ward, Beighton, Sheffield, in April 1968.

Britannia Class 4-6-2 No. 70023 *Venus*

With little time left, an engine, once very smart but now a mess, heads north at Winwick Junction with an afternoon parcels in 1967. The shed plate and the name have gone, and the number and name are hand painted. The Riddles-designed engine was built at Crewe Works in August 1951 and allocated to 81A Old Oak Common. After a busy but not overly long life, it was withdrawn from 68A Carlisle Kingmoor in December 1967 and cut up at T. W. Ward, Killamarsh, four months later. This was another engine that can be found as a Hornby oo scale model.

Coronation Class 4-6-2 No. 46238 *City of Carlisle*

One of the beautiful greyhounds of the rail network, this once-'crimson lake'-coloured shiny locomotive heads north at Leyland 1963. Outside scrap yards, it would have been difficult to find an engine so decrepit and dull. No. 46238 *City of Carlisle* was designed by William Stanier and built at Crewe Works in September 1939. It was one of the engines that was streamlined until nationalisation, when the streamlining was removed. Its first and last shed was 12A Carlisle Upperby, from where it was withdrawn in September 1964 and cut up at Arnott Young, Troon, three months later.

Jubilee Class 4-6-0 No. 45600 *Bermuda*

No. 45600 *Bermuda* is seen here at the head of a parcels train in Manchester Victoria in 1965. I have included it as the view of the station and the clarity of the photograph would be a shame to miss.

WD 2-8-0

We encounter yet another absolutely filthy WD 2-8-0 locomotive as it heads north at Winwick Quay in 1963. Known also as 'Austerities', these were built for the War Department during the last war. In total, 935 were built, making them one of the biggest classes of locomotive. Most were built to a design by R. A. Riddles at the North British Locomotive Works in Glasgow. After the war they went to various destinations; the majority ended up with British Railways but others could be found around the world. Three were retained by the War Department at the Longmoor Military Railway. Only one was named, and that was *Vulcan*, after the Vulcan Foundry. Just one was preserved and that one was repatriated from Sweden by the K&WVR.

Black Five No. 45156 *Ayrshire Yeomanry*

It is August 1968, the last month of regular steam on BR, and one of only four named Stanier Black Fives stands in a bay at Manchester Exchange. *Ayrshire Yeomanry* was built at Armstrong Whitworth in July 1935 and in 1948 could be found at 65B St Rollox shed. It was withdrawn in August 1968 from 24B Rose Grove and cut up at T. W. Ward, Beighton, Sheffield, four months later. I say four named Black Fives, but there were originally five, the fifth being No. 45155 *The Queen's Edinburgh*, which had the name removed in 1944. Some preserved Black Fives have been named, but only No. 45154 *Lanarkshire Yeomanry*, No. 45157 *The Glasgow Highlander* and No. 45158 *Glasgow Yeomanry* were named and retained their names until withdrawal. None were preserved.

Black Five 4-6-0 No. 44874

What a good shot of a 1960s railway platform with a steam engine waiting the right away with its excursion. The place is Manchester Victoria and the year is 1968, when sights such as this were coming to an end. Stanier Black Five No. 44874 was built at Crewe Works in April 1945 and four years later could be found allocated to 5A Crewe North. Its last shed was 11A Carnforth, from where it was withdrawn in August 1968, the last month of steam, and cut up at Drapers, Neptune Street, Goods Yard, Hull, in March 1969.

9F 2-10-0 No. 92047

It is a wet day in Crewe station during 1965 as a sturdy ten-year-old 9F stands ready to head north with a long freight train. The Riddles-designed engine was built at Crewe Works in February 1955 and allocated to 15A Wellingborough. Its last shed was 6C Birkenhead, from where it was withdrawn in November 1967 and cut up at Campbell's of Airdrie in April of the following year. Nine of these relatively modern steam engines have been preserved and the last one, No. 92220 *Evening Star*, was built at Swindon Works during March 1960 and withdrawn exactly five years later. It is now a static exhibit at the National Railway Museum at York.

Ivatt Class 4MT 2-6-0 No. 43041

The large stadium and towering spotlights of Manchester United's Old Trafford ground are in the background as Ivatt Class 4MT 2-6-0 No. 43041 passes by on a dull day in 1963. The locomotive easily manages the short train of coal wagons and a guard's van. Designed by H. G. Ivatt, it was built at Horwich Works for BR in August 1948 and withdrawn from 24C Lostock Hall in August 1967. It was cut up at Clayton & Davie, Dunston on Tyne, four months later. This class numbered 162 and only three were built before nationalisation in 1948. They were quite well thought of engines, especially the high running plate that made servicing easier, but despite this and their relatively short lives, only one, No. 43106, was taken into preservation and is now operational at the Severn Valley Railway.

Ivatt 2-6-0 No. 43031

One of the more modern workhorses of the branch lines was this class of BR locomotives. It is seen here entering Heaton Mersey station in 1964. This station was closed in 1961, but local trains from Manchester Central continued to stop there until it finally closed in 1967. There is nothing left of the station today; even the cutting has been filled in and the line is no more. As for the Ivatt-designed engine, it entered service in April 1949, having been built at Horwich Works, and in 1952 it could be found at 14A Cricklewood East. Its last allocation was to 13C Heaton Mersey, from where it was withdrawn in March 1966 and in the same month it was cut up at the Central Wagon Company, Ince, Wigan.

9F 2-10-0 No. 92070

This is Trafford Park shed in Manchester during 1965, where we find simmering quietly a well-worked 9F No. 92070. This engine was only built at Crewe Works during January 1956 and was then allocated to 36A Doncaster, making it around nine years old at the time of the photograph. Despite this short life, it was to be withdrawn about two years later on 30 November 1967 from 6C Birkenhead Mollington Street and cut up at Campbell's of Airdrie three months later. This locomotive was built with a single chimney and was fitted with a high-sided tender.

Jubilee Class 4-6-0 No. 45664 *Nelson*

Northbound at Winwick Junction in 1963, travelling light engine, is Jubilee No. 45664 *Nelson*. The locomotive was built in January 1935 at Derby Works and in 1948 it could be found at 13A Trafford Park. Its last shed was 8B Warrington Dallam, from where it was withdrawn in May 1965 and delivered to Drapers, Neptune Street, Goods Yard, Hull to be cut up.

Class 5 4-6-0 No. 45037

A look now at a good example of the grit and grime that went with steam in those far-off days as Black Five No. 45037 is back in the area of its first allocation on nationalisation, 10C Patricroft. It passes Patricroft station box in 1962 with a mixed train, including coal wagons and box vans. It was built at the Vulcan Foundry in 1934 and went into service in September of that year. It was withdrawn from 5D Stoke in November 1965 and scrapped two months later at Cashmore's of Great Bridge. Patricroft station is still there but now as an unmanned halt.

Class 5s 4-6-0 No. 44780 and No. 45206

A typical train spotter's shot now of Manchester Victoria station in 1968, almost the last day of main line steam, and these chaps make the most of a scene that would soon disappear. There are two Black Fives, and the first one at the platform with its strange train of mixed stock is No. 44780. This locomotive was built during July 1947 at Crewe Works and in 1948 was allocated to 26A Wakefield. It was withdrawn from 26A Newton Heath on 30 June 1968 and scrapped at Cohen's of Kettering, Cargo Fleet four months later. The second engine is No. 45206, seen trundling through the station with steam to spare. It was built by Armstrong Whitworth, entering into service in June 1935. On nationalisation, it was also allocated to 26A Wakefield and was withdrawn from 10A Carnforth at the end of steam in August 1968. It was scrapped by Cohens, Cargo Fleet, in December of that fateful year.

Unnamed WD 2-8-0

Another typical steam-era photograph and an interesting view of the lineside bothys and brick-built sheds that could at one time be found all over the network for assorted employees of the railway company. This is Patricroft station on a misty day in 1962 as a WD 2-8-0 with plenty of steam hauls its mixed goods train through this once busy station. The station is not quite as busy now but still serves the people of Eccles, albeit with multiple units.

9F 2-10-0 No. 92127

Another look at the Manchester United Old Trafford football ground as 9F No. 92127 takes a freight past in 1962. Built at Crewe Works, this engine entered service on 30 April 1957 and was allocated to 15A Wellingborough. After just ten years, three months and one day, it was condemned on 31 August 1967 while at 8H Birkenhead Mollington Street and scrapped three months later at Buttigiegs of Newport.

Britannia Class 4-6-2 No. 70044 *Earl Haig*

Southbound at Leyland in 1963 is the Britannia Class 4-6-2 *Earl Haig*. Turned out of Crewe Works in June 1953 and allocated to 9A Longsight, it was not named until 1957 and could be seen in the 1950s with no windshields as it was used to test experimental airbrake equipment. This equipment was sighted at the front of the smokebox, where the windshields would normally be. Its last shed was 9B Stockport Edgeley, from where it was withdrawn in October 1966. It was cut up in February 1967 at T. W. Ward, Beighton. It is preserved as a oo gauge Hornby model.

8F 2-8-0 No. 48313

It's that freezing winter of 1963 as 8F No. 48313 heads a heavy freight through Thelwall station near Warrington. Snow covers the station but apart from the draughts, the driver and fireman will have been quite warm. The engine was built at Crewe Works during December 1943, but unlike some of the class built during the war years, it went straight into service with the LMS. On nationalisation, it was to be found at 18A Toton and on 7 January 1967, it was withdrawn from 9K Bolton. During the last month of steam in 1968, it was scrapped at Cashmore's of Newport.

2 X 9F 2-10-0 No. 92016

Newton Heath shed in 1967 with two powerful 9Fs sitting in the yard – the one in the foreground is No. 92016. This was built at Crewe Works and went into service in October 1954, being allocated to 15A Wellingborough. Its last shed was 10A Carnforth, from where it was withdrawn on 17 June 1967 for scrapping during April 1968 at J. McWilliams of Shettleston.

5MT No. 44674

Here we see another member of the ubiquitous Black Five class of Stanier engines southbound at Leyland in 1963. It was built in March 1950 at Horwich Works and it was withdrawn in December 1967 from 68A Carlisle Kingmoor. It was cut up at T. W. Ward, Inverkeithing, on 31 March 1968.

8F No. 84712 heading south towards Warrington in 1966

A mixed view here, with an iconic 8F engine hauling a mixed freight towards Warrington and passing a builder's yard containing a period Ford Consul and a Ford Prefect or Anglia. The 2-8-0 locomotive was built at Brighton Works during July 1944 and, unlike a lot of its class members, it did not go into War Department service. On amalgamation, it was allocated to York with the shed code YK but, after a period on loan to Crewe, it was soon reallocated to 9D Buxton. On 13 May 1967 it reached its final shed, 24L Carnforth, from where it was withdrawn the following month.

Fowler 0-6-0 No. 44365

South of Winwick Junction and north of Warrington in the late 1950s, and we find one of the ubiquitous Fowler engines, No. 44365. It is heading a mixed freight tender first with a well-stoked fire. The engine was built at Andrew Barclay & Sons, Kilmarnock, in 1927 and went into service in May of that year. On nationalisation, it could be found allocated to 9D Buxton, and on 30 November 1959, it was withdrawn from 12D Workington, from where it went to Crewe Works for scrapping in January 1961.

A1 Pacific 4-6-2 No. 60154 *Bon Accord*

No. 60154 *Bon Accord* simmers in the sun at Neville Hill shed in Leeds on 29 August 1965. Designed by the last CME of the London & North Eastern Railway Arthur Peppercorn, the locomotive was built at Doncaster Works in September 1949 and allocated to 58A Gateshead. Its last shed was Leeds Neville Hill, from where it was withdrawn on 4 October 1965 and scrapped at T. W. Ward Beighton, Sheffield, the following month. Bon Accord is the motto of the city of Aberdeen and is French for 'good agreement'. There is also a town of Bon Accord in Canada, which takes its name from the Aberdeen motto.

Black Five 4-6-0 No. 44675

The water spraying from beneath the wheels tells us that the engine is drawing water from a trough between the rails, in this case Moore water troughs as the Black Five heads north towards Warrington in 1965. The short mixed goods does not tax the Stanier engine at all; it was built at Horwich Works and entered into service on 31 March 1950. One of the last Black Fives to be built, it had upgrades designed by George Ivatt such as outside Stephenson link motion and Timken roller bearings. Its last shed was 68A Carlisle Kingmoor, from where it was withdrawn on 30 September 1967 and scrapped six months later at Motherwell Machinery and Scrap, Inslow Works, Wishaw.

Britannia Class 4-6-2 No. 70049 *Solway Firth*

An engine at speed, No. 70049 *Solway Firth*, caught heading north towards Warrington with the afternoon parcels in 1966. Named after the Solway Firth in Scotland, this engine was built in July 1954 at Crewe Works and first allocated to 6J Holyhead. After many shed changes across the network, its last shed was 12A Carlisle Kingmoor, from where it was withdrawn on 9 December 1967 and scrapped at J. McWilliams, Shettleston, three months later.

Black Five 4-6-0 No. 45156 *Ayrshire Yeomanry*

Another look now at one of the only named Black Fives – the details are already available on page 63. This one gives us a good insight into the early days of container use on BR; *Ayrshire Yeomanry* is passing through Manchester Exchange station in 1968 with a long train of Conflat A wagons and containers. As it is travelling tender first, it is more than likely that it is simply on shunting duties. Again, the ubiquitous train spotter is present.

A4 4-6-2 No. 4498 *Sir Nigel Gresley*

A visitor to the Cheshire area, we see on Moore water troughs A4 No. 4498 *Sir Nigel Gresley*. Still within the steam era, but already preserved, the photograph was taken in 1967 as it passed through Cheshire on an enthusiasts' special. It was built in October 1937 at Doncaster Works having been designed by its namesake, Sir Nigel Gresley. Its first allocation was KX King's Cross, and on nationalisation, it was at 35B Grantham. Its last shed was 61B Aberdeen Ferryhill, from where it was withdrawn in February 1966. It was saved from the cutter's torch by the newly formed Sir Nigel Gresley Locomotive Preservation Trust Ltd, a name that was later shortened. In 1967, it carried out a number of rail tours when painted in LNER Garter Blue. After this, BR banned steam on main lines until 1972. Since 2015, the locomotive has been in the Railway Museum at York being overhauled.

4F 0-6-0 No. 44460 and 9F 2-10-0

We are in Leeds Holbeck yard now as the old and the new sit simmering together. No. 44460 was built at Horwich Works in May 1928, having been designed by Henry Fowler. On nationalisation, it could be found at 24A Accrington, and it was withdrawn from 26A Newton Heath on 31 October 1964. On 28 February 1965, it was cut up by T. W. Ward, Killamarsh. The number of the 9F is not known.

4F 0-6-0 No. 44460

We are staying with No. 44460 now in order to enjoy the period vista of Holbeck MPD in Leeds. The shed was opened by the Midland Railway on 9 May 1868 and closed to steam on 2 October 1967. Prior to this, it was an important and very busy engine shed. Fortunately, it went on to be an important diesel shed albeit having been cut down in size, and with many buildings demolished, it is now a shadow of its former self.

Brittania Class 4-6-2

This photograph has been included to show just how run down engines were allowed to become as the last day of steam approached. This train is being pulled by a once proud greyhound of the rails, a Britannia class engine. Its number and name are unknown as it passes Dallam shed in Warrington. It is filthy and devoid of nameplates as it hauls a mundane train of assorted stock northbound in 1964.

8F 2-8-0 No. 48399 and Fowler 2-6-4 tank No. 42409

Still at Leeds Holbeck shed in 1963, and we see 8F No. 48399, an engine that was built at Horwich Works during June 1945; on nationalisation, it could be found at 15C Leicester. It was withdrawn in October 1966 from 9J Agecroft and scrapped in February 1967 by Drapers Ltd of Hull. The Fowler, No. 42409, was built in October 1933 at Derby Works and in 1948 was at 25F Low Moor. It was withdrawn from this shed in January 1964 and scrapped at Darlington Works, North Road, the following month.

Jubilee Class 4-6-0 No. 45589 *Gwalior* and No. 45675 *Hardy*

Another Leeds Holbeck photograph in 1963, showing a brace of Jubilees in the form of first No. 45589, which was built at the North British Locomotive Works, Glasgow, in December 1934 and allocated to this shed on nationalisation. Its last shed was 25A Wakefield, from where it was withdrawn in March 1965 and scrapped at Cashmore's of Great Bridge one year later. The second Jubilee, No. 45675, was built at Crewe Works in December 1935 and in 1948 could be found at 5A Crewe North shed. Its last shed was this one, from where it was withdrawn on 31 July 1967 and scrapped at Cashmore's of Great Bridge four months later.

Patriot Class 4-6-0 No. 45512 *Bunsen*

The Springs Branch Wigan signal box with rebuilt Patriot No. 45512 *Bunsen* posing on the line leading to the shed in 1963. A Fowler-designed engine built in September 1932 at Crewe Works with a parallel boiler, it was allocated to 5A Crewe North in 1948. It was rebuilt to a taper boiler design by Ivatt in July 1948; the rebuild included a double chimney and new cylinders. Its last shed was 68A Carlisle Kingmoor from where it was sent to the Motherwell Machinery and Scrap at Inslow Works, Wishaw, to be cut up in July 1965.

Standard Class 4 2-6-0 No. 76084

It is 1964 as No. 76084 trundles northbound near Winwick Junction, north of Warrington, with a small mixed goods. Although the engine is decidedly scruffy and ill-kempt, it was one of the lucky ones that was later preserved. Designed by R. A. Riddles and built at Horwich Works in April 1957, it was just seven years old at the time of the photograph. Allocated to 24D Darwen, it was withdrawn from 10A Wigan Springs Branch in December 1967, the last BR Mogul to be withdrawn. Taken to Barry Scrapyard with other members of the class, an attempt to rescue it in 1974 failed, and it remained there until 1982. It was purchased for £7,500 and taken to Nottingham where it languished in its purchaser's back garden. On the death of the owner in 1997, the newly formed No. 76084 Locomotive Company Ltd purchased it as a cosmetically prepared engine. Over the next sixteen years, it was restored, and it can now be seen on the main line again in shining lined black and in beautiful condition, a credit to the owners.

Coronation Class 4-6-2 No. 46256 *Sir William A. Stanier FRS*

Another look at my favourite engine as it stands at Crewe in 1963 with a good fire in the boiler and plenty of smoke.

Ivatt Class 2 2-6-0 No. 46512

A busy Crewe station in 1963 is the location for this photograph as No. 46512 passes down one of the centre lines, while an unnamed Warship Class diesel waits at the platform with a train for the South. No. 46512 was designed by Ivatt and built at Swindon Works in December 1952 and was another one of the lucky ones to go into preservation. It was allocated to 89A Oswestry. Its last allocation was 5B Crewe North, from where it was withdrawn in December 1966 and sent to Woodhams Brothers scrapyard in June 1966. It was rescued from there in 1982 and rebuilt at Aviemore. The engine is now in first-class condition on the Strathspey Railway (below) and is called *E. V. Cooper Engineer*, after the engineer who led the long restoration of the engine.

9F 2-10-0 No. 92081

It is 1964 as No. 92081 travels with a light engine northbound through Winwick Junction. The Riddles-designed engine was built at Crewe Works in May 1956 and allocated to 18A Toton. It was withdrawn from 26A Newton Heath on 28 February 1966 and scrapped at W. George, Station Steel, Wath on Dearn, in June 1966.

Royal Scot Class 4-6-0 No. 46115 *Scots Guardsman*

We saw earlier photographs of *Scots Guardsman* in excellent condition; here we see it in less-than-such condition at Winwick Junction in 1962. It is showing plenty of smoke as it pulls a mixed goods northbound.

Patriot Class 4-6-0 No. 45527 *Southport*
Staying at Winwick Junction on the same day, we see a rebuilt Patriot Class engine for the second time in the book, also travelling northbound. Looking very similar to *Scots Guardsman*, but a different class, it also has the honour of pulling a passenger train and not a mundane goods like the Royal Scot.

WD 2-8-0 No. 90316
A big, ugly, battered but powerful engine from the War Department pulling an unfitted freight northbound out of Warrington in 1962. Designed by R. A. Riddles and built by the North British Locomotive Works in March 1944 for the War Department, it later entered BR stock in 1948. Its last shed was 38A Colwick, from where it was withdrawn in December 1965, and on 30 April 1966, it was cut up at Drapers, Neptune Street, Goods Yard, Hull.

Standard Class 4 2-6-0 No. 76079

Standard Class 4 No. 76079 proceeds southbound at Winwick Junction in 1962. We have already learned the story of how it was preserved and how it is now in the fleet of the North Yorkshire Moors Railway. But this photograph depicts it as a hard-working engine with a mixed goods.

Jubilee Class 4-6-0 No. 45705 *Seahorse*

Here Stanier Jubilee No. 45705 *Seahorse* takes a short ballast train northbound at Winwick Junction in 1963. The engine was built at Crewe Works in May 1936, and on nationalisation, it was allocated to 25G Farnley Junction. Its last shed was 26A Newton Heath, from where it was withdrawn in November 1965 and cut up the following month at Cashmore's of Great Bridge.

Jubilee Class 4-6-0 No. 45556 *Nova Scotia*

A Jubilee in a rather good condition is seen heading southbound at Moore in 1964. No. 45556 *Nova Scotia* has a short train of containers and vans. The engine was built at Crewe Works in June 1934 and in 1948 could be found at 9A Longsight. Its last shed was 5A Crewe, from where it was withdrawn on 5 September 1964; on 1 January 1965 it was cut up at Birds of Morriston. The bricked-up tunnel that can be seen in the centre of the photograph was the Acton Grange Railway tunnel. It was 108 yards long and on the line from Warrington Bank Quay to Moore. It was opened in 1888 and closed in 1893 when the line was deviated, as can be seen in this shot.

Class 5 4-6-0 No. 45106

Seen near Leyland, travelling northbound in 1965, is a leaky engine nearing the end of its useful life. Black Five No. 45106 was one of the oldest of this massive class of Stanier engines. It was built at the Vulcan Foundry in May 1935. In 1948, it could be found at 12A Carlisle Upperby, and its last shed was 68A Carlisle Kingmoor, from where it was withdrawn in January 1967 and scrapped at Campbell's of Airdrie in May of the same year.

Jubilee 4-6-0 No. 45736 *Phoenix*

Staying at the same location and date as the last photograph, we find Jubilee No. 45736 *Phoenix* with plenty of steam to spare and in slightly better condition than the last. The engine was built at Crewe Works in November 1936 and, on nationalisation, could be found at 1B Camden. Its last shed was 68A Carlisle Kingmoor, from where it was withdrawn on 26 September 1964, and on 31 January 1965 it was cut up at Hughes Bolckow, Battleship Wharf, North Blyth.

Jubilee 4-6-0 No. 45580 *Burma*

Another Jubilee, *Burma*, at Winwick Quay, north of Warrington in 1965; the driver and fireman relax as the engine sits quietly across the lines. The engine was built at the North British Locomotive Works, Glasgow, in October 1934. It was allocated to 68A Carlisle Kingmoor on nationalisation, and its last shed was 26A Newton Heath, from where it was withdrawn on 12 December 1964. In April 1965, it was cut up at T. W. Ward, Beighton, Sheffield.

Crewe Works visit 1966

For anyone interested in trains during the steam era of full sheds and works, a visit to one of them was a treat not to be forgotten. Accordingly, we will look at one here: it was a visit by Phil to Crewe Works in 1966. In this first photograph, we see the yard on an open day with enthusiasts and notebooks mingling among the locomotives. Most in this shot are diesels that are starting to usurp the steam and would soon completely take over. The Class 52 Western locomotive in the foreground of the three Westerns is, I believe, D1001 W*estern Pathfinder*, which was built in Swindon Works in December 1961 and withdrawn in February 1974 to be scrapped at Swindon Works in August 1977.

Crewe Works visit 8F 2-8-0 No. 48096 in 1966

In this shot, we see 8F 2-8-0 No. 48096 minus tender outside the workshop. The engine was built in December 1938 at Crewe Works, and its first shed under nationalisation was 16C Kirkby in Ashfield. It was withdrawn in October 1965, so although it looks quite smart, its days were numbered. I can find little information on the demise of this engine and the reason for its withdrawal after apparently visiting the paint shop.

Crewe Works visit 9F 2-10-0 No. 48096 in 1966

In the workshops now, and what do we find but a very rough-looking engine that was the only 9F that bore a name from new: *Evening Star*. In 1966, the engine was just six years old, and what was it doing in Crewe Works having what looks like a major overhaul? It was the very last steam engine to be built by BR. The engine was designed by R. A. Riddles at Brighton and built at Swindon Works in March 1960. Unlike the rest of the class, it was painted in BR Brunswick green livery and given a copper-capped double chimney. The name *Evening Star* was chosen after a competition in 1959/60 by BR Western Region staff. As a result, a special commemorative plate was and is attached under the name on the windshields. It reads,

> No. 92220 built at Swindon, March 1960, The last steam locomotive for British Railways. Named at Swindon on March 18, 1960 by K. W. C. Grand, Esq, Member of the British Transport Commission.

9F locomotives were designed for heavy freight but *Evening Star*, being rather special, could be found on express passenger services and prestigious named trains in and around the Western Region. Its use on flagship express passenger trains came to an end when senior management of BR started to worry about the effect that these high speed duties were having upon what was after all an engine not designed for high speed express work. The engine that had been earmarked for preservation since it was built was withdrawn on 31 March 1965 at the ripe old age of five years. But what then? The engine had been withdrawn from Cardiff East Dock. In 1966, the engine had been simply left and as a result was in a poor state. It was towed via Shrewsbury to Crewe Works, where we find it in this unique photograph undergoing a heavy repair to prepare it for preservation.

It has been steamed since leaving the works but most of its time has been spent as a static museum exhibit. It is now performing such a duty at the National Railway Museum at York.

Crewe Works visit 9F 2-10-0 No. 92150 in 1966

Back out to the works yard, and we find a good-looking 9F that seems to have been in the wars, with many dents on view. Despite this, it seems to have had the attention of the paint shop. No. 92150 was built to R. A. Riddles' design at Crewe Works in October 1957, and its first allocation was to 18B Westhouses. Its last shed was 25A Wakefield, from where it was withdrawn on 30 April 1967 and scrapped at Drapers, Neptune Street, Goods Yard, Hull, three months later.

Crewe Works visit 1966 Standard Class 2 2-6-0 and Black Five

Another look at the yard as two locomotives are seen part way through having work completed. The far one is a Standard 2-6-0, a class that was built between 1952 and 1956. Then, nearer to the camera, a Black Five in primer paint. These sort of repairs and overhauls were going on up to the end of steam.

Crewe Works visit 2-10-0 9F No. 92138 and Britannia 4-6-2 No. 70054 in 1966

The enthusiasts are surging across the lines and gather around No. 92138. This locomotive was built in 1957 at Crewe Works and posted to 21A Saltley. Its last shed was 8C Speke Junction, from where it was withdrawn on 31 July 1967 and scrapped at Birds of Long Marston five months later. The second identifiable engine in the distance is No. 70054 *Dornoch Firth*. This engine was built at Crewe Works in September 1954 and allocated to 66A Polmadie. It was withdrawn from 68A Carlisle Kingmoor on 26 November 1966 and scrapped at Motherwell Machinery and Scrap, Inslow Works, Wishaw, six months later.

Jubilee No. 45563 *Australia*

This well-worn Jubilee is seen on lowly shunting duties at Bank Quay station, Warrington. The locomotive was built at the North British Locomotive Co. in 1934, going into service in August that year. In 1949, it could be found at 10C Patricroft and it was finally allocated to 8B Warrington Dallam in September 1963. It was withdrawn shortly after this image was taken on 27 November 1965 and scrapped in March of the following year at Cashmore's of Great Bridge.

Coronation No. 46250 *City of Lichfield*

A nice close-up shot of this Coronation class engine, which gives a snapshot of a life when steam ruled the rails, with the driver enjoying his morning cigarette. No. 46250 *City of Lichfield* is at Winwick Quay with a northbound parcels train in 1963; this may have been a bit of a come down from the purposes for which it was originally built.

Jubilee No. 45595 *Southern Rhodesia*

Jubilee No. 45595 *Southern Rhodesia* is seen here laying down a smoke screen at Moore while travelling southbound in 1965. The engine was built at the North British Locomotive Co. in Glasgow during January 1935. In 1948 it was at 12A Carlisle Upperby, while its last shed was 5A Crewe North. It was withdrawn from there on 30 January 1965 and, on 31 May, it was cut up at Cashmore's of Great Bridge.

8F 2-8-0 No. 48108

It's 1965, north of Warrington, and this grubby 8F trundles past the Winwick Quay signal box. It was built at Crewe Works during February 1939 and, on nationalisation, it was allocated to 16C Kirkby in Ashfield. Its last shed was 9L Buxton and, in August 1967, it was condemned.

Britannia Class 4-6-2 No. 70006 *Robert Burns*

An action shot here of an unusually well-kept Britannia in the powerful form of No. 70006 *Robert Burns* as it heads north at Winwick Quay in 1965. The engine was built in April 1951 at Crewe Works and allocated to 31A Stratford. Its last allocation was 68A Carlisle Kingmoor, from where it was withdrawn in May 1967. It was then cut up at J. McWilliams, Shettleston, in October 1957. Another engine that can be found as a oo gauge model in the Hornby stable, it was also manufactured by Dapol in N gauge.

Britannia Class 4-6-2 No. 70039 *Sir Christopher Wren*
It was late 1963 and *Sir Christopher Wren* is northbound at Leyland, in a worn condition, but still with its nameplates and the shed plate, 12A, together with the 'SC' Self Cleaning plate. The engine was built in February 1953 at Crewe Works and allocated to 32A Norwich Thorpe. Its last shed was 68A Carlisle Kingmoor, from where it was withdrawn in September 1967 and cut up at J. McWilliams, Shettleston, two months later.

5MT 4-6-0 No. 45108
It's the West Coast Main Line at Moore near Warrington, as Black Five No. 45108 heads southbound in 1964. The engine was built in May 1935 at the Vulcan Foundry in Newton-le-Willows. In 1948 it could be found at 5B Crewe South; its last shed was 10A Wigan Springs Branch, from where it was withdrawn in December 1965. It was cut up by Central Wagon Co., Ince, Wigan, in April 1966.

Crosti-Boilered 9F 2-10-0 No. 92025 and Black Five No. 45046

It's 1966 and we are in Edgeley, Stockport, as two engines in steam are on the yard. 9F No. 92025 is in a rather beaten-up condition – even the smokebox number is handwritten. This locomotive was built at Crewe Works during June 1955 and, as mentioned earlier, it was a 9F but in a small experimental sub class, which, as it transpired, was not a great success. It was allocated to 15A Wellingborough and its last shed was 16C Birkenhead. It was withdrawn on 30 November 1967 and cut up at Campbell's of Airdrie on 30 April 1968. The far engine, No. 45406, was built at the Vulcan Foundry in October 1934, while in 1948 it was in 12A Carlisle Upperby. Its last shed was 26C Bolton, from where it was withdrawn on 30 June 1968 and cut up at Cohen's of Kettering in November of the same year.

Hughes / Fowler Crab 2-6-0 No. 42777

Seen at Moore, south of Warrington, and heading towards Chester in 1963 is a 2-6-0 Fowler Crab, No. 42777. George Hughes was the CME of the Lancashire & Yorkshire Railway and the LMS, while Henry Fowler was his deputy at the LMS, later becoming CME himself. The locomotives, nicknamed 'Crabs', were originally designed by Hughes; this one was built at Crewe (not Horwich) during August 1927 and in 1947 it could be found at 2B Nuneaton. Its last shed was 6C Birkenhead, from where it was withdrawn on 14 August 1965 and cut up at Birds of Long Marston in March 1966.

Standard Class 5 No. 73142

Back to Warrington Bank Quay for a nice crisp shot and plenty of smoke as No. 73142 departs the station with a southbound train in 1965. The train will not be stopping here as it is on a through track, and Joseph Crosfield's soap works can be seen in the background. The engine, with Caprotti valve gear, was built at Derby Works in November 1956 and allocated to 15C Leicester Midland. Its last shed was 10C Patricroft, from where it was withdrawn in April 1968 and cut up at Cashmore's of Great Bridge in September of that year.

Fowler 4F 0-6-0 No. 44300

An engine from the ubiquitous Class 4F heads north at Winwick Junction in 1965. Its train of mixed goods is in the slow lane as a more prestigious working comes down the main line with a steam engine in charge. The Fowler was built at Derby Works in February 1927 and, on nationalisation, allocated to 5B Crewe South. Its last shed was 11A Carnforth, from where it was withdrawn in December 1965 and scrapped at T. W. Ward, Beighton, Sheffield, two months later.

Britannia Class 4-6-2 No. 70013 Standard Class *Oliver Cromwell*

We could not end this book without a look at the most important of the engines that worked the last month of main-line steam. Unlike the Black Fives and Standaards that also worked the last of the specials in the fateful last days of August 1968, *Oliver Cromwell* and two of its three Black Five partners were not thanked by being summarily scrapped. The Ivatt-designed locomotive was built at Crewe Works during May 1951 and allocated to 32A Norwich Thorpe, with its last shed being 11A Carnforth. It was withdrawn from BR on 17 August 1968. *Oliver Cromwell* was the lead locomotive on the famous Fifteen Guinea Special. This train was the last one to run on BR metals before a ban was imposed to start on 12 August 1968. This was an expensive treat for the enthusiasts who could afford it. The special from Liverpool to Carlisle via Manchester Victoria and was hauled from Liverpool to Manchester by Black Five No. 45110, which was preserved and can now be found on the Severn Valley Railway, named *RAF Biggin Hill*. *Oliver Cromwell* took over the train from Manchester to Carlisle and then for the return two Black Fives double headed, taking over for the trip back to Manchester. These were Nos 44781 and 44871; the latter was preserved and is at the East Lancashire Railway. No. 44781 was not so lucky, as it was derailed for the film *The Virgin Soldiers* and scrapped on site.

At Manchester Victoria, Black Five No. 45110 took over and hauled the train back to Liverpool. That was thought at the time to be the last-ever steam working on British Railways, apart from the Vale of Rheidol, until it was privatised. The one permission that BR did give was for *Oliver Cromwell* to return to its old shed at Norwich and Diss on 12 August under its own steam to go into preservation. The steam engine had been the last one to receive a full service at Crewe Works. It is now owned by the National Railway Museum.

Hughes/Fowler crab No. 42732

Now for a truly interesting shot, taken from a rather precarious place on the tender of one of the Hughes/Fowler Crabs, No. 42732, as it heads southbound at Winwick Quay in 1965. The engine was designed by George Hughes, CME of the LMS, and put into service by his successor Henry Fowler. The name 'Crab' comes from the look of the engine in comparison to a crab's pincers and also the feeling on the footplate that the engine was 'scuttling' along the tracks due to the inclined cylinders. They were also called Horwich Moguls. This engine was built not at Horwich but at Crewe Works in December 1926 and was allocated on nationalisation to 25F Low Moor. Its last shed was 24D Lower Darwen, from where it was withdrawn in June 1965 and scrapped at T. W. Ward, Killamarsh, three months later.

Jubilee Class 4-6-0 No. 45604 *Ceylon*

No. 45604 gets the signal to proceed southbound while north of Warrington in 1963 with its train of vans. The engine was built in March 1935 at the North British Locomotive Works at Glasgow, and on nationalisation it was at 20A Leeds Holbeck. Its last shed was 26A Newton Heath, from where it was withdrawn in July 1965 and scrapped at Cashmore's of Great Bridge three months later.

8F 2-8-0 No. 48476 and Standard 5MT 4-6-0 No. 73069 with BR Class 25 Diesel No. D7513

It is the last day of main line steam working on BR metals, and these three coupled engines await their tour of duty on a special train for enthusiasts. The date is 4 August 1968, the last day of BR steam, and the two steam engines have travelled down from Lostock Hall MPD to Manchester Victoria, where they can be seen here. The tour, 1L50, was organised by the Railway Correspondence and Travel Society as the 'End of Steam Commemorative Rail tour'. There were many hiccups such as the 8F being in quite a poor condition and having to be taken off the train at Blackburn, and it was said that the Standard had to pull the train and push the 8F for a lot of the way! It was replaced with a scruffy Black Five No. 45407, all was forgiven and, despite this, a good time was had by all. The 8F was built at Swindon Works from 1943 to 1945. The day after the rail tour it was withdrawn and was scrapped later on in the year. The Standard 5MT, No. 73069, was built in November 1954 at Crewe Works and was allocated to 17A Derby. Its last shed was Carnforth, and it was withdrawn from there on 31 August 1968 and scrapped at Cashmore's, Newport, in March 1969. It has been preserved as a oo scale model by Bachman Branchline models.

The BR Type 2 Bo-Bo Class 25 Diesel, No. D7513, was built at Derby Works and introduced in November 1964. It was later given a TOPS No. 25163. It was first allocated to 16A Nottingham and withdrawn from Crewe Diesel in November 1980 and cut up at BREL Swindon in March 1983.

Black Five 4-6-0s Nos 45017 and 44874

And, finally, there were many excursion specials on the last days of steam; pictured here on Sunday 4 August 1968 is one of them. It was a Stephenson Locomotive Society special (1Z79) 'Farewell to Steam Rail Tour' from Manchester Victoria to Huddersfield, returning via Copy Pit. The tour itself started and finished in Birmingham New Street but these engines covered the length that was powered by steam traction.

The engine was built at Crewe Works during May 1935 and was allocated to 68A Carlisle on nationalisation. Its last shed was 11A Carnforth, and it was withdrawn during August 1968 and scrapped at Drapers, Neptune Street, Goods Yard, Hull, on 30 April 1969.

The lead engine 4-6-0 No. 44874 was built at Crewe Works in April 1945 and could be found at 5A Crewe North in 1948. Its last shed was 11A Carnforth, and it was withdrawn during August 1968 and scrapped at Drapers Street Goods Yard, Hull, on 31 March 1969.

Both engines here are in excellent cosmetic condition and that was almost certainly due to the actions of enthusiasts.